© Ingrid van Amsterdam, September 2017

INTRO

- In May 2017 I was asked to do a talk about buying property in New Zealand one evening at a meeting with Migrant Connections Taranaki. I came up with the idea to put together an easy to read booklet for migrants thinking about buying property, to take home as a quick and easy reference. At the time I was working as a qualified real estate sales consultant (REAA 2008) in New Plymouth with Western First National Real Estate. I would like to thank and acknowledge Sonja Barrett (trustee at Migrant Connections Taranaki) for inviting me as guest speaker on the night, and Alex McDougall (Sales Manager, Western First National Real Estate) for some pointers on the presentation.

- Being a migrant myself having come to New Zealand in 1988, I understand some of the challenges one may face getting used to a new country. I had to learn and understand terms not previously heard of or learnt with my "school English"! And in the real estate world you may find that some of the terms may have different meanings from country to country. In fact the purchasing process for real estate may be quite different from one country to another, so understandably this can be confusing. In this booklet you will find terms explained and defined in easy to read bullet points, in chronological order of the purchase process.

- I was pleased to find that my booklet was very well received by all migrants who attended on the night, as well as the members present from Migrant Connections Taranaki and Citizens Advice Bureau. I found that not only is this booklet very useful to migrants ('this is exactly what I needed when I came to New Zealand but there wasn't such a thing when I moved here") but also for our fellow Kiwis ("this would have made the process of buying my property so much easier") and I hope that this will help make your property purchase experience a pleasant one.

Ingrid van Amsterdam

PROPERTY TYPES

- Leasehold
- Cross lease
- Freehold

LEASEHOLD

- An interest in land that is less than freehold, owning the building but not the land.
- Having the right to possess or occupy a property for a limited time as stated in the lease document and may be renewed.
- Ground rent and council rates apply.

CROSS LEASE

- This has the elements of a Freehold and a Leasehold estate where the lease is long term.
- A number of owners have an undivided share of a Freehold property, giving each owner ownership rights of the undivided section.
- Each owner has possession rights to a specified portion of the property.
- No lease fees are payable.
- The land owners of a Cross lease are tenants in common and must give their approval before any work which changes the footprint of a building e.g. alterations, additions or demolition as this will change the site plan on the Certificate of Title.
- The lease is between the owners, while having an undivided share of the total land area.

FREEHOLD

- The owner of a freehold property has the right to decide to sell, gift, mortgage, trade or leave it to a beneficiary by will.
- A freehold property is potentially of infinite duration.
- The owner also has other rights such as build, subdivide, or lease the property within local council guidelines.

REAL ESTATE AND LAW

- REAA (Real Estate Agents Act) 2008 amended 2011
- Privacy Act
- Fair Trading Act
- OIA (Overseas Investment Act)

REAA 2008

- The salesperson is supervised and directed by the agent to ensure the work carried out is done competently and in accordance with their rights and obligations as set out in the Act.
- The agent's license allows the licensee to carry out real estate agency work and is authorised to sell or offer any land by auction, provided that the licensee is competent and sufficiently skilled or experienced to do so.
- The salesperson attends regular training to keep up to date with the real estate laws and practices in New Zealand.
- REAA is a government agency. Real estate agents and salespersons are accountable to them.

PRIVACY ACT

- No personal/private information can be passed on or disclosed without that person's written consent.

FAIR TRADING ACT

- No-one in trade can be associated or involved in behaviour or acts that are (likely to be) misleading or deceptive.
- Anyone in trade involved with sales or advertising property needs to be certain they have all the details correct. Even a mistake could be perceived as false or misleading representation.

OIA - OVERSEAS INVESTMENT ACT

- Applies to "overseas persons" wishing to purchase "sensitive assets" in New Zealand.
- Consent must be obtained from the Overseas Investment Office to purchase or take control over sensitive assets in New Zealand.

OVERSEAS PERSONS

- A non NZ Citizen or someone not usually living in New Zealand.
- A company or body corporate incorporated outside NZ.
- A company, body corporate or partnership incorporated in NZ where 25% or more of any class shares is owned or controlled by an overseas person.

SENSITIVE ASSETS

- Non-land business assets worth more than NZ$100 million
- Rural property with a land area of over 5 hectares
- Land on most off-shore islands
- Certain property with a land area of over 0.4 hectares e.g. on
    - some islands
    - including or next to a reserve
    - land adjacent to parks, sports grounds etc.
    - Conservation Act land
    - land with historic or heritage areas
    - certain lakes
- Land over 0.2 hectares including or next to the foreshore

REAL ESTATE SALE METHODS

- Auction
- Tender
- Private treaty

AUCTION

- To offer a property up for bid, taking bids and sell it to the highest bidder.
- If a reserve price has been set the bid has to meet or exceed the reserve price.
- The customer needs to have the necessary consents with regard to the Land Settlement Act, the Overseas Investment Act, and local body requirements or restrictions e.g. resource and building consents and matters covered in the LIM report.
- The property is sold at the fall of the hammer and a bid cannot be withdrawn.
- A deposit of 10% has to be paid immediately after the fall of the hammer.

TENDER

- The property owner invites offers in a closed envelope (a confidential offer) from prospective buyers.
- An offer may be conditional or unconditional.
- It is the prospective buyer's responsibility to inspect the property, make enquiries, or obtain specialist advice such as a building inspection, LIM or registered valuation.
- A tender cannot be withdrawn until five working days after the closing of the tender.
- A prospective buyer makes his own decision with regard to the value of the property and any conditions of sale required.
- The amount offered must be specific.

PRIVATE TREATY

The purchaser deals directly with the seller, normally through an agent.

- Single offer
- Multi offer
- Back up offer
- Conditional offer

SINGLE OFFER

- Only one prospective purchaser makes an offer which may be conditional or unconditional.

MULTI OFFER

- More than one prospective buyer put in an offer on a property.
- The offers are presented together to the vendor, each offer presented in a sealed envelope.
- A prospective purchaser may not get the opportunity to negotiate.

BACK UP OFFER

- An offer which is made after an existing conditional agreement is already in place.
- The back up offer can only be considered if the existing agreement doesn't meet its conditions and can then be negotiated, declined, or accepted. This is subject to the initial offer being served notice that they have so many days to declare their offer unconditional. If this doesn't happen, the second (back up) offer goes into place.

CONDITIONAL OFFER

- An offer which is subject to any conditions needing to be fulfilled.
- An agreement may contain conditions inserted by a prospective buyer as well as a prospective seller, e.g.
    - an offer may be made subject to the buyer selling their house within a certain time frame.
    - a buyer may request that certain repairs take place by a qualified tradesperson.
    - a seller may sell their property on condition that they will find a new house by a stated date.
- Conditions protect both the prospective client and purchaser.

PLEASE NOTE:

- A property can be sold prior to closing date if advertising states that the property "can be sold prior". This applies to both auction and tender methods.
- Real estate sales are conducted by private treaty, accounting for 93% of all sales in Taranaki.
- Based on current figures approximately 5% of property is sold by auction and 2% by tender in Taranaki (statistics provided by REINZ).
- Private treaty is a normal process conducted by using a standard Sale and Purchase Agreement.

Percentages stated as per May 2017 in the Taranaki region and may be subject to change.

SALE & PURCHASE AGREEMENT COMMON CONDITIONS

- LIM report
- builders report
- methamphetamine report
- OIA
- subject to finance
- solicitor's approval as to title
- settlement date
- unconditional date

LIM REPORT

- "LIM" stands for Land Information Memorandum.
- Provides information on specific properties, obtained from council records held at the local authority (e.g. NPDC - New Plymouth District Council in the New Plymouth region).
- Contains information on planned use, rates, sewerage, and stormwater.
- Shows what building consents or code compliance certificates have been issued.
- Can include information of historic or potential erosion, debris and flooding on the property.

BUILDERS REPORT

- Shows you the condition of the building on the property e.g. weather tightness or signs of rotting timber or sunken piles.
- Will tell you if repair is recommended.

METHAMPHETAMINE REPORT

- It is now common practice for a prospective buyer to request a methamphetamine report.
- A clear report will ensure the buyer that the property tested is not contaminated and will be of specific interest if a property is bought for the purpose of renting.

OVERSEAS INVESTMENT ACT

Refer to **OIA** under **'REAL ESTATE AND LAW'**

- You should always check with your lawyer if the Overseas Investment Act applies to you and whether you need to obtain consent from the Overseas Investment Office.

SUBJECT TO FINANCE

- A buyer may put an offer in on a property, provided that he will have sufficient funds to purchase the property.
- If finance is needed this should be approved by an approved lender.

SOLICITORS APPROVAL AS TO TITLE

- A common condition inserted into a Sale and Purchase Agreement to protect the purchaser with respect to any encumbrances or other interests registered against the title of the property (e.g. the property is still under an existing mortgage).

SETTLEMENT DATE

- The settlement date is the date when the balance of the purchase amount is paid.
- Is usually the same date as the possession date.

UNCONDITIONAL DATE

- This is the date when all the conditions (clauses) in the Sale and Purchase Agreement have been met.
- The property is then legally SOLD.

THE DEPOSIT

- The deposit on a property is paid once the sale and purchase agreement becomes unconditional.
- The deposit is held for a minimum of 10 working days in the agent's trust account before being released.
- The initial deposit is usually 10% of the purchase price or an amount agreed between the parties.

NEGOTIATION

- Both the vendor and the purchaser have the right to negotiate the offer made.
- The negotiation process usually involves the salesperson who will discuss the possibilities, making the process less stressful for both parties.

THREE STEPS TO SUCCESS

1. ALWAYS GET A SOLICITOR
2. Check you are qualified and have finance approved if needed
3. Due diligence

1. SOLICITOR

- Always get legal advice.
- A solicitor has specialist knowledge and understanding of property law and will be able to explain to you all the fine details.
- You will be protected and misunderstanding prevented.

2. ARE YOU QUALIFIED?

- Affordability - Loan needed? - Approved lender
- Deposit 20% needed - LVR (Loan to Value Ratio) is set to 20% of the purchase price for a private dwelling and 40% for an investment dwelling. (As per May 2017 and may be subject to change)

3. DUE DILIGENCE

- Determining if a property is fit for purpose - What is the property used for and does it fulfil the criteria?

DECISION TIME!

- You have checked all the details
- Crossed the "t's" and dotted the "i's"
- Does the property match your criteria?
    - No - keep looking
    - Yes - time to put pen to paper!

PUTTING PEN TO PAPER

- Time to sign an Offer/Agreement Form, stating:
    - The address you wish to purchase
    - Your personal details (name & contact details)
    - Your solicitor
    - The purchase price (your offer)
    - The deposit and if finance is needed
    - Chattels
    - Settlement date
    - Conditions
- Now you are ready to sign a Sale and Purchase Agreement (in New Plymouth this is mostly done by Private Treaty)

SALE AND PURCHASE AGREEMENT

- Once you have signed a Sale and Purchase Agreement it is ready to be presented to the vendor.
- The vendor can now consider your offer and decide to:
  - Decline - no further negotiation
  - Negotiate - counter offer
  - Accept your offer!
- Once all parties (both the vendor and purchaser) have signed the agreement you have an agreement and the property is now **Under Contract** until all conditions have been fulfilled and the agreement becomes **Unconditional.**
- Marketing can now cease and you are officially the owner of your new home!

THE UNCONDITIONAL AGREEMENT

- All conditions have been fulfilled
- The balance is paid on settlement date
- Settlement date usually is also **possession date**
- Possession date is the date you are handed the keys to your new home

CONGRATULATIONS, YOU ARE NOW OFFICIALLY THE OWNER OF YOUR NEW HOME!

NOTES

www.ingramcontent.com/pod-product-compliance
Lightning Source LLC
Chambersburg PA
CBHW040311220526
45473CB00002B/636